CULT CLASSICS

MUSIC FROM CULT FILMS ARRANGED BY RICHARD HARRIS · FLUTE AND PIANO

© 2002 by Faber Music Ltd
First published in 2002 by Faber Music Ltd
3 Queen Square London WC1N 3AU
Cover by Velladesign
Music processed by Don Sheppard
Printed in England by Caligraving Ltd
All rights reserved

ISBN 0-571-52103-7

To buy Faber Music publications or to find out about the full range of titles available
please contact your local music retailer or Faber Music sales enquiries:

Faber Music Limited, Burnt Mill, Elizabeth Way, Harlow, CM20 2HX England
Tel: +44 (0)1279 82 89 82   Fax: +44 (0)1279 82 89 83
sales@fabermusic.com   www.fabermusic.com

FABER *ff* MUSIC

Pulp Fiction 1994 Directed by Quentin Tarantino

Starring John Travolta, Samuel L. Jackson, Uma Thurman and Harvey Keitel

Pulp Fiction
Misirlou

Words and music by Milton Leeds,
N. Roubanis, Fred Wise and Bob Russell

©1942 Campbell Connelly and Company Limited, 8/9 Frith Street, London W1. Used by permission of Music Sales Ltd.
All rights reserved. International copyright secured.

Diva 1981 Directed by Jean-Jacques Beineix

Starring Fredric Andrei, Wilhelmenia Wiggins Fernandez and Richard Bohringer

Diva
'Ebben ne amorò lontana' from *La Wally*

Alfredo Catalani

©2001 by Faber Music Ltd.

8

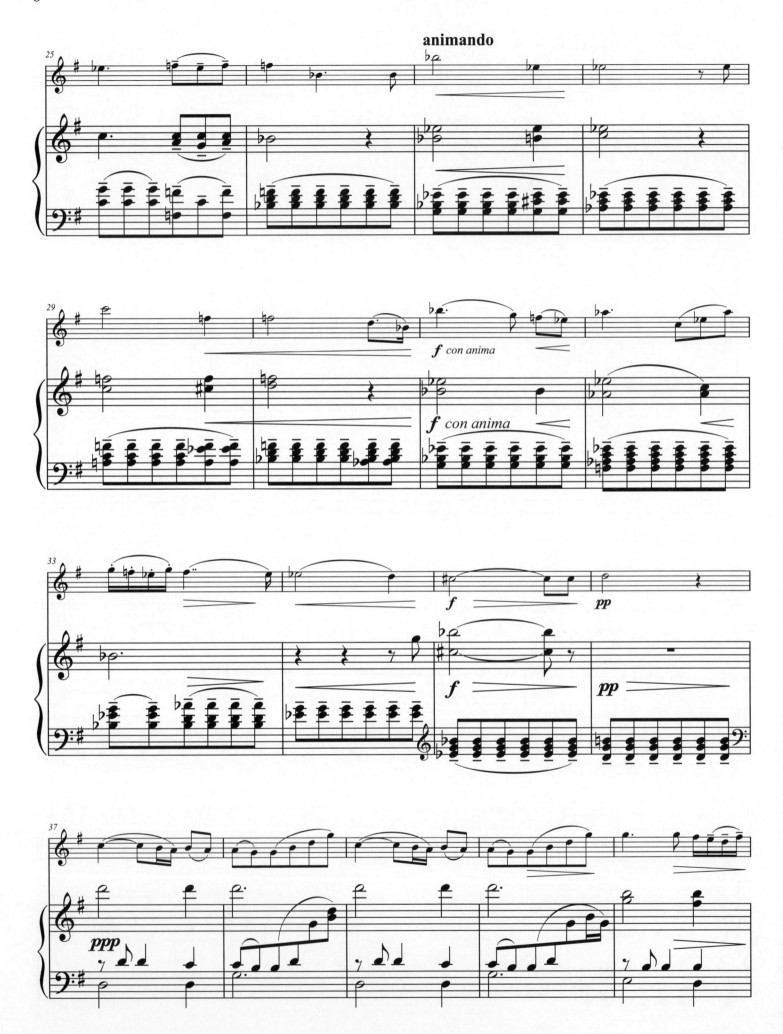

Shadow of the Vampire 2000 Directed by E. Elias Merhige
Starring John Malkovich and Willem Dafoe

Shadow of the Vampire
A Concert in Wismar

Dan Jones

©2001 by Dan Jones. All rights administered by Rights Worldwide Ltd.

Die Hard 1988 Directed by John McTiernan
Starring Bruce Willis and Alan Rickman

Die Hard

First movement from *Brandenburg Concerto* No. 3

Johann Sebastian Bach

©2001 by Faber Music Ltd.

Flute

Pulp Fiction
Misirlou

Words and music by Milton Leeds,
N. Roubanis, Fred Wise and Bob Russell

©1942 Campbell Connelly and Company Limited, 8/9 Frith Street, London W1. Used by permission of Music Sales Ltd.
All rights reserved. International copyright secured.

Diva

'Ebben ne amorò lontana' from *La Wally*

Alfredo Catalani

©2001 by Faber Music Ltd.

Shadow of the Vampire
A Concert in Wismar

Dan Jones

©2001 by Dan Jones. All rights administered by Rights Worldwide Ltd.

Die Hard

First movement from *Brandenburg Concerto* No. 3

Johann Sebastian Bach

©2001 by Faber Music Ltd.

Trainspotting

'Habañera' from *Carmen*

Georges Bizet

©2001 by Faber Music Ltd.

Reservoir Dogs

Little Green Bag

Hans Bouwens
and Jan Visser

©1969 Veronica Music and EMI Music Publishing (Holland) BV. EMI Music Publishing Ltd, London WC2H 0QY.
Reproduced by permission of International Music Publications Ltd. All rights reserved.

Fatal Attraction

'Un bel di' from *Madama Butterfly*

Giacomo Puccini

Andante molto calmo ♩= 48

©2001 by Faber Music Ltd.

Apocalypse Now

'The Ride of the Valkyries' from *Die Walküre*

Richard Wagner

©2001 by Faber Music Ltd.

CULT CLASSICS

MUSIC FROM CULT FILMS ARRANGED BY RICHARD HARRIS · FLUTE AND PIANO

© 2002 by Faber Music Ltd
First published in 2002 by Faber Music Ltd
3 Queen Square London WC1N 3AU
Cover by Velladesign
Music processed by Don Sheppard
Printed in England by Caligraving Ltd
All rights reserved

ISBN 0-571-52103-7

Trainspotting 1995 Directed by Danny Boyle
Starring Ewan McGregor, Ewen Bremner, Jonny Lee Miller and Robert Carlyle

Trainspotting

'Habañera' from *Carmen*

Georges Bizet

©2001 by Faber Music Ltd.

Reservoir Dogs 1992 Directed by Quentin Tarantino
Starring Harvey Keitel, Tim Roth, Chris Penn and Steve Buscemi

Reservoir Dogs
Little Green Bag

Hans Bouwens
and Jan Visser

©1969 Veronica Music and EMI Music Publishing (Holland) BV. EMI Music Publishing Ltd, London WC2H 0QY.
Reproduced by permission of International Music Publications Ltd. All rights reserved.

Fatal Attraction 1987 Directed by Adrian Lyne
Starring Michael Douglas and Glenn Close

Fatal Attraction
'Un bel di' from *Madama Butterfly*

Giacomo Puccini

©2001 by Faber Music Ltd.

Apocalypse Now 1979 Directed by Francis Ford Coppola

Starring Marlon Brando, Martin Sheen, Robert Duvall, Dennis Hopper and Harrison Ford

Apocalypse Now
'The Ride of the Valkyries' from *Die Walküre*

Richard Wagner

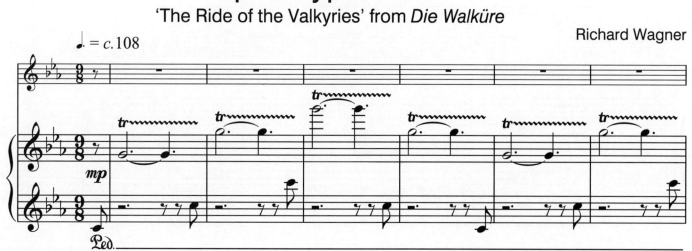

©2001 by Faber Music Ltd.